Usborne
Phonics Readers
Big pig on a dig

Phil Roxbee Cox
Illustrated by Stephen Cartwright
Edited by Jenny Tyler

Language consultant: Marlynne Grant
BSc, CertEd, MEdPsych, PhD, AFBPs, CPsychol

There is a little yellow duck to find on every page.

First published in 2006 by Usborne Publishing Ltd., Usborne House, 83-85 Saffron Hill, London EC1N 8RT, England. www.usborne.com
Copyright © 2006, 1999 Usborne Publishing Ltd.

Big Pig gets a letter.

Look for this hat.

Big Pig

Big Pig sees the hat.

There is a map in the hat.

Big Pig runs
to Fat Cat.

4

"Fat Cat! Look at the map in this hat."

"It shows where to dig, Fat Cat."

5

"Where to dig?
Dig for what,
Big Pig?"

"Gold!" grunts Big Pig.
"Old gold."

"But I am a cat.
Cats need to nap.
I am a napping cat."

"You dig, Big Pig.
Be a pig on a dig."

7

"Let me nap

and dream of cream."

8

Big Pig sees three green trees.

Big Pig sees three green trees on the map.

Big Pig is happy.

He pops on a wig.

Big Pig is happy.

He hops on a twig. He can go on a dig!

"I am a happy big pig on a dig."

"I dig down

and down

and...

13

What has Big Pig found...

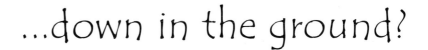

...down in the ground?

It's Funny Bunny.

"There's no old gold here."

Big Pig grins. "Digging is fun too!"